The Missing Chapters:
AN EPILOGUE TO
THINK & GROW RICH

The Missing Chapters:

AN EPILOGUE TO
THINK &
GROW RICH

*Discover the Three Key Principles
Missing from the Classic Publication by
Napoleon Hill*

PAUL MARTINELLI

Contents

INTRODUCTION

<u>Chapter 1</u>

Every story has a beginning, a middle, and an end.

Most "beginnings" are full of hope. Those feelings one experiences at the birth of a child, how that new life represents unexpressed possibility that is starting to bud from within. There is a lightness, an excitement, and a certain joy and anticipation in the new beginnings of a story. Well, at least most of the time, I should say.

And then there is the "middle" of the story. So often, as the middle approaches and takes over, the hope and joy of the beginning slips away into nothingness, and the middle is characterized by drudgery, monotony, regret, and forgotten dreams.

And the interesting thing about the middle is that you never really know at what point you pass from the middle and enter into the "end" until it is too late, until all the sand in the hourglass has passed through, and those unfulfilled hopes and dreams are laid to rest forever.

So, let me tell you a story that is still being written. This story has a beginning, and it has a middle, but the end has not yet passed. It is still being written and I acknowledge it to be a work in progress. What you must know is that, within this story, there is the progressive realization of the hopes and the dreams that I believe are seeded at conception in the core of every human being, as their own story begins.

But perhaps, what is worth noting most of all, and what makes the telling of this story a worthwhile endeavor, is that if you were to only read the first half of this story, you would never know that there are indeed hopes and dreams being developed, nurtured, cultivated, and grown, just below the surface for many, many years. For this story defies convention—the convention that hope usually turns into the regret that marks the ultimate end of an unlived dream. And the reason this story defies convention is because, as a human being, resourced with infinite creative ability, and with a spiritual essence that seeks fuller expression and fuller expansion, I chose to defy convention. Sometimes, I wondered if it was divine intervention or if it was my own personal act of harnessing my inner power that gave me the wherewithal to defy what most people accept as fate. I have found that perhaps it was a little of both. Most likely, a combination of the two.

If the conventional beginning of a story is one of hope and expectation, then let it be known that, upon the outset of this story, there was no hope. It held no anticipation and no joyful expectation. This is a story of dark beginnings.

It begins at 430 Coolidge Avenue in Pittsburgh, Pennsylvania. The home of my upbringing. A house of terror for my three siblings and me.

In my many years of teaching in the field of personal growth and human potential, I have been hesitant to share the details of these early years of my life, lest it hit a nerve with you, and also to protect the person who was the primary cause of the terror inflicted on my siblings and me. Quite frankly, the details would give chills to even the most cold-hearted of individuals.

So, at the risk of causing undue pain, let me bare a piece of my heart to you in hopes that it will open your eyes, your heart, and your mind to a deeper level of awareness of the secrets that I have discovered and seek to share with you within these subsequent chapters to provide my own perspective, trusting that it will be the tuning fork that resonates to your truth and awakens within you an understanding of who and whose you are.

So, as I was saying, 430 Coolidge Avenue was a house of terror.

It was the impoverished home of a single mom—my mother—and her four children, Jeannie, Tom, David, and me. My father left my mother when she was three months pregnant with me. When looking in from the outside, it was like any other middle-class home, actually in one of the wealthier suburbs just outside the city of Pittsburgh. But as we all know, looks can be deceiving.

And although I know pieces of my mother's story, and I know that she experienced a very difficult and troubled upbringing, one where she was harmed, neglected, bullied, and abused, I still cannot in any way fully fathom how and why she perpetrated that same level of abuse on my three siblings and me. No matter the difficulties of one's childhood, that can *never* provide excuse for a person to perpetrate any degree of harm on another human being.

As an adult now, I see children with their parents; I see the love expressed from mother and father to child, and it is inconceivable to me how any human being could be capable of exacting pain and terror upon someone as innocent as a child. But indeed, my mother was capable.

I have memories of lying in my bed as a small boy of four or five years of age, hearing my mother raging in the kitchen below, breaking every dish in the house. And I would just lie there, staring into the pitch black of my bedroom, my stomach beginning to tie itself in anxious knots, sometimes wetting the bed from fear, dreading the inevitable sound of her storming up the stairs toward the rooms where my siblings and I were cringing in our beds. She would beat us. Not every day, but enough days to feel those emotions right now as I write this as a fifty-four-year-old man.

I would come home from school, and I would never know what person I would meet on the other side of that front door. Some days, she was loving and doting, promising to make us cookies or to play with us (promises that were almost always unkept). And other days, the person I encountered inside my home had no resemblance to what a mother should be. She was dark, distant. My little mind could feel with its intuition the rage she had boiling and building inside her, as she would lie on the couch, not saying a word—just fuming. And we would resign ourselves to waiting for the inevitable explosion, trying not to make a sound lest we be the cause of it.

I remember one winter's night, waking up to my mother pulling me by my hair out of bed and dragging me down the stairs, my body flailing side to side, hitting the walls as I tried to grab with one hand the railing to stop her, and with the other, holding her hand tight against my head so she wouldn't rip my hair out of my scalp. Once we hit the bottom landing, it was the slide across the living room carpet and then onto the cold linoleum floor. I can still remember thanking God for the slippery surface of the linoleum as my small body could be dragged along it more quickly, making the time held in her grip shorter. And then I was tossed through the aluminum storm door and out onto the snow and ice covered back porch.

Wintertime in Pittsburgh is cold—freezing, in fact. She would throw my siblings and me outside, threatening to lock us out until one of us confessed to the supposed misdeed of moving her comb set. Although I couldn't say how long we were really out there, it felt like hours, huddling together in the blistering cold. It was all we could do to try to share our body heat, to keep each other warm and alive. There we were, three small boys, ages five, nine, and eleven (my sister had already left to live with my grandparents after my mother's sometime-live-in lover tried to sexually assault her, but that's a different story…) in shock, freezing, too scared to call out for help and too frightened to dare raise a defense. Praying, maybe, maybe not—I'm not sure if silent begging is the same as prayer.

Holidays for children of abuse are not filled with joyful expectation; they are filled with fear. One of my mother's favorite go-to forms of abuse was the build-up/let-down scenario. She would build our hopes for something and take great joy in retracting it from us. I remember when I was eight years old, spending an unusually happy day decorating the Christmas tree, with the promise of watching the annual holiday specials, like *Frosty the Snowman*, *How the Grinch Stole Christmas!*, and *A Charlie Brown Christmas*, only to have her fly into a rage for some rule violation like not closing the kitchen cabinet, and then spending the rest of the night taking all the ornaments off the tree and dragging the tree to the backyard. Hopes destroyed. Expectations crushed. And lips punched swollen.

This was the home of my upbringing.

Now, when most children begin to speak around the ages of one or two years old, I did not. Perhaps it was because there was no predictability to the behavior of my mother, and any given word or deed could seemingly set her off. And so, for the sake of self-preservation, I kept my mouth shut. Or maybe it was as simple as the fact that my small body was besieged with stress and anxiety every single day. And the havoc this wreaked on my mental, emotional, and physical development prevented me from learning this essential function of human communication.

As I gradually grew older, I slowly began to open my mouth and develop my ability to speak. However, as I tried to do so, I developed a debilitating stutter. Not a single word or phrase would leave my mouth that I wouldn't hear someone laughing at me, teasing me, and calling me dumb and stupid.

This was back in the late 1960s and early 1970s. Back then, a speech impediment was considered a learning disability. Teachers and educators simply did not understand what we now know to be true: that, in fact, the vast majority of stuttering problems are a result of some form of trauma, and not at all due to learning disabilities. But because of the lack of awareness at that time, I was immediately labeled slow and disabled.

On the playground of life, kids can be cruel. And the kids at my school had a field day with me. "Hey d-d-d-dummy…. Hey st-st-st-stupid," they would call out every day as I walked past the schoolyard, on my way to and from school, and during every recess and lunch hour out on the playground.

I remember, every day around ten o'clock in the morning, the school secretary's voice would sound over the PA system: "Please send Paul Martinelli down to the special education classroom." As I stood up from my desk in my homeroom class, I would hear the snickers and laughter from my classmates. And as a five-, six-, seven-, eight-year-old, what do you think this did for my self-image and my self-esteem?

You have to understand something about the development of a child's self-image and belief system. From the very moment our life begins, each one of us is programmed to believe certain things about ourselves, about our world, about our potential, about the potential of others, about what is possible, and about what we can and cannot do. And until the age of seven to nine years old, which is when most kids begin to form the ability to reason, we take anything that is told to us and we accept it as truth. Not just any truth, but *our* truth. As those kids were calling me dumb and stupid, day after day after day; as those teachers were instilling in me that I was slow and that I couldn't learn; as my mom would compare me to my siblings and make comments that I would never be as smart as them and I would never amount to anything (I was SEVEN years old), that is what I internalized as *my* truth, and it formed the core of my self-image and my self-belief.

When you believe a certain thing to be true, it shows up in your behavior, period, end of story. Our beliefs drive our behavior.

So, how do you think a little kid who believes himself to be dumb and stupid will behave and act? Of course, in a way that proves this belief to be true and that serves to reinforce it further. It was a vicious cycle, seemingly unending and unbreakable. I believed it to be true. The kids all around me told me it was true. My mom berated me with comments that it was true. My teachers had lower expectations of and for me, and I rose only to those lowered expectations. I didn't pay attention in school—after all, what's the point if I can't learn anyways? I started skipping classes. And I failed test after test after test. And through all of this, I simply reinforced for myself the belief over and over again that I was indeed dumb and stupid.

I created a learning model of marginalizing myself and diminishing myself. I would actually say things about myself, like "when God was handing out brains, I was first in line, but then I had to hold the door for everyone else." This kind of self-deprecating humor was not humor at all; it was a brilliant model of self-preservation. I would say hurtful things about myself first, so you wouldn't need to. What a brilliant strategy to protect myself emotionally.

At the ripe old age of sixteen, I dropped out of high school. Although, truthfully, that is to put it kindly. I was called into the principal's office and told in so many words that my educational career was coming to an abrupt halt because, based on my current trajectory, I would not graduate high school for at least four more years. Apparently, Mount Lebanon High School did not favor having twenty-year-olds in attendance.

That was the day I also found out that, in my home, the day you drop out of school is also the day you move out. And I found myself kicked out of my home and sleeping on the floor of a karate school that I had joined years before. Once again, my behavior proved that what I believed about myself must be true: that I was dumb, that I was stupid, that I couldn't learn, and that I would never amount to anything.

This first part of my life was characterized by struggle. I was living a disempowered life of victimhood, operating under the guise that all of these conditions and circumstances had happened to me. If my spirit would ever dare to begin to dream, my negative self-esteem and my low self-image would immediately kick into high gear and allow that ego-centered voice of self-judgement, of programmed limiting beliefs, to speak up and smother any hope of a better future…"Who do you think you are?" "How are you going to do that?" "What makes you think you're so special?"

My self-talk was filled with the limiting linguistic metaphors of "money doesn't grow on trees," "the rich get richer and the poor get poorer," "you have to just play the cards you're dealt," "beggars can't be choosers," "damned if you do, damned if you don't," "a day late and a dollar short." And the limiting beliefs thus represented filled my internal dialogue and were the filter of my thinking for the first half of my life.

Does any of this sound familiar? These voices of our limiting beliefs are so cunning. They tell us things that sound reasonable and believable and congruent with what life has taught us up to this point. Of course, money doesn't grow on trees. Who do I think I am? Nothing…I am nothing, and I am good for nothing.

That vicious cycle continued to persist in my life.

Shortly before I was kicked out of high school, and while studying karate, I learned of an organization called the Guardian Angels. This was a group primarily comprised of underprivileged youth who had been brought together and organized by the founder, Curtis Sliwa, with the greater purpose of fighting crime in New York City and other metropolitan centers of the United States. In the worst neighborhoods of America, where even the police were too trepidatious to enter, the Guardian Angels would patrol, and they would valiantly fight crime perpetrated against innocent victims.

At this point in my life, I was very much a lost soul. I was living aimlessly, trying to find something to grab hold of, something that would give me purpose and meaning. When I learned of the Guardian Angels, I immediately joined forces and poured myself into it with everything I had. This was the first time in my life that I felt like I was doing something right, like there was a reason for my existence.

As I worked diligently to increase the impact of the Guardian Angels, I slowly moved my way up the ranks until I was working as the right-hand man to Curtis

Sliwa himself. For several years, this was my life. I went on the road to open new chapters of the Guardian Angels in other American cities, and I felt like I was really making a difference. We were protecting lives and serving people every day.

But as is the case for all people of every race and color and culture and creed, we seek more. We seek to express ourselves in greater and more expansive ways. We are spiritual beings, after all, created for fuller expression and fuller expansion. And as much as my work in the Guardian Angels had fed me up to that point and had set my life on a new and much more positive trajectory, something was stirring in my soul, a longing to be, do, and have more.

During this time, I had also been working a dead-end job as a roofer earning minimum wage. I was terrified of heights, but this was the best thing I figured I could do. My work with the Guardian Angels provided me with some purpose for my life, but it did not pay my bills. I continued to live in financial struggle. I spent day after day after day up on the roof, working in the blazing sun, just wishing and wanting to have a new life, a better life.

I would wake up early every day to go to a job I hated. I would stand at the bus stop at five o'clock in the morning, and, while on the bus going to the job I hated, I prayed they would not fire me. Again, the voice of those limiting linguistic metaphors served as a filter for my thinking…"This is as good as it gets. Play the hand you've been dealt."

If wishing and wanting could get you the life you desired, I would have been a billionaire by the time I was twenty years old. But, instead, I was miserable. As Napoleon Hill very clearly articulates in the original text of *Think and Grow Rich*, you must have a burning desire. Wanting and wishing will never achieve. I had been so beat down all my life, and told I would never amount to anything so many times, that it took everything in me to begin to look beyond that into the great world of possibility.

All dreams begin as a seed, and once that seed is planted and watered and nourished and cultivated, it begins to sprout and grow roots. At the time, I didn't understand this truth. I was just slowly beginning to imagine that perhaps there was a better life for me, but I didn't know how to cultivate and develop the seed of that dream.

I would be up on the roof, talking to Tony, who was working right there beside me, and I would begin to tell him about my ideas for a business. I would ask Tony what he thought. And the problem was, Tony didn't think. Tony's thinking had gotten him to the exact same place in his life as my thinking had gotten me—right there, stuck on the roof.

Make sure that when you ask someone what they think, you first determine that they actually do think, that their level of awareness exceeds your own, and that they will be able to speak into your life in a meaningful way. How often have you sought the opinion and the approval of others without even realizing that those people are just as stuck as you are?

I remember when I was about twenty-two years old, sitting down for Thanksgiving Day dinner at my mother's house. At that table were my mom and stepfather, my two brothers, my Uncle Pete (my mom's older brother), and my grandmother. My grandmother was the love of my life. Through all the trauma of my upbringing, my grandmother had been my rock. I loved her dearly, and she was my one source of security and steadiness. I valued her opinion above all others.

"I think I'm going to start a cleaning company," I blurted out all of a sudden. *Clink* went the sound of each fork hitting the plates of those sitting around the table. My whole family looked at me. In a split second, their faces showed the undisguised shock and disapproval that they felt, and then it started. "What? How are you ever going to do that? You, a cleaner? Don't you remember how your room looked growing up? No one would ever hire you. What do you know about business? Where are you going to get the money to start? In this economy?" (*It was 1988, and the country was in a recession.*) And on and on it went. My grandmother suddenly looked up from her plate as if she had just had a brilliant idea. "Call Ro, call Ro. Maybe she can get him in."

"Ro" was my cousin, Rose, who worked at the Post Office. My grandmother's grand plan for my life was that maybe my cousin Rose could get me a job as a mail carrier. That was the best my grandmother could imagine for my life. These were my partners in belief! Let me tell you something right now: If you leave the fate of your life up to the imagination of others, be prepared for a small life.

Quite truthfully, I do not know how I found it within myself to persist beyond their ridicule and disbelief. But again, that spiritual essence in me, that part of me and you that is always seeking fuller expression and fuller expansion, fought all those voices coming from within and from without, and, despite the collective disapproval of everyone around me, I made the decision to take the only two hundred dollars I had to buy a used vacuum cleaner, a mop, and some furniture polish and go into business for myself, cleaning offices late at night.

I had no idea how it would work out, but I knew I needed something more. At twenty-two years of age, I decided to move to Florida permanently and put all of my energy into this new endeavor. I was all in.

But those voices never go away. The self-judgement. The self-ridicule. "Who do you think you are?" "How are you going to do that?" "You don't know anything about business." "High school dropouts don't get rich."

Regardless, I pressed forward. Persistence triumphed.

Two years into this business, I had built it to the point where I was making twenty thousand dollars a year (which was a big leap from when I was working on the roof with Tony). And then I got stuck. Up until that point, things were going pretty well for me. I thought everything was going to keep growing. And then, suddenly, it stopped. Everything I did to grow the business seemed to work against me. I would get a new client account, and two would drop off. I would buy a new piece of equipment only to have several other machines break down. I would hire a new employee, and the next day someone would quit. I was that proverbial hamster on the wheel, picking up speed and going nowhere.

You see, it was all rooted in those belief systems. Do you want to know why I started a cleaning company? Well, because I figured any dummy could clean a toilet, and I was any dummy. It wasn't because I had a dream of being "Mister Clean." One way or another, sooner or later, the limiting beliefs you hold onto are bound to catch up with you. They certainly did for me.

I tried everything I could think of, as well as taking the advice of everyone around me, to get my business to start to grow again. I lowered my prices. I raised my prices. I changed my marketing. I paid my employees more. I put in more hours. It didn't matter. None of it worked. Because the problem wasn't in the behavior; the problem was in the belief.

And then, one fortuitous day, everything changed. Now, don't be mistaken. The appearance of things did not all change on that day, but the truth is not always in the appearance of things. There was one small shift that happened, a one-degree change to the trajectory of my life, almost imperceptible. It is like a pilot going off course by a single degree when departing London, England for New York, setting her in an entirely different direction so she ends up in Miami or elsewhere; in a similar way, a slight shift in the *right* direction can mean the difference between living a life of struggle until your dying day or experiencing the fullness and abundance of the life I believe we are all created to live.

I remember so clearly the day I walked into that office for the first time. It was a small business in the middle of a strip mall in North Palm Beach, Florida. I was making cold calls in the area, drumming up more clients for my cleaning business. I walked in and looked around. It was all very average. A couple of old desks. Some papers littered on top. Worn chairs in the reception area.

On the sign above the door was written, "Ideas and Things." This was certainly a strange name for a business, but, nonetheless, I thought, "Okay. Let's give it a shot." And in I walked. As the door closed behind me, I heard a voice call out from one of the back rooms, "Hello!! I'll be right there!"

I don't know why I picked that street on that day and walked through that door of that business, but I would be remiss not to say that perhaps Divine Intervention played more of a role than some might give it credit for.

The man who walked out of the back room and came toward me looked almost like your average, middle-aged man in South Florida. And yet different. He was a good-looking guy, with silver fox hair. But he was wearing a Hawaiian shirt and a pair of casual shorts; there was a rope necklace with a seashell pendant hanging around his neck, flip-flops on his feet, and his look was completed with about seventeen different wristbands up his wrist, all for different campaigns—save the trees, save the whales, save the turtles…if something could be saved, he was all in for saving it. He was somehow like a cross between a mad professor and your average Caucasian American—almost looking like a dropout from the 1960s Woodstock. I looked around. There was nothing special about the office in which I was standing. Nothing that would indicate to me that this man walking toward me would provide me with the answers that I did not even know I was seeking. I had zero inkling as to how this one encounter would change the rest of my life forever.

"Hey, what can I do for you?" he asked me. He was happier, friendlier, just a bit more interested and engaged than most people I talked to and met with on a daily basis. There *was* something a little different about this guy.

I started in, asking him if he had a cleaning company that serviced his office. As I talked, I looked around again. If someone was indeed cleaning his office, then, in my personal and professional opinion, it was time to fire them. This was going to be an easy sell, I told myself.

He chuckled at one point as I was in the middle of my pitch and held up his hand. "Okay, okay, that sounds good. You can clean my office…but I think I might be able to help you as well."

I tilted my head to one side, slightly taken aback. Someone was actually offering to help *me???* I was so accustomed to the idea that if I was going to make anything of my life, I had to be self-reliant and I couldn't count on a single other human being.

Maybe he knew something about the cleaning business. I was in a slump, after all. Things weren't going so well. And what I did know was that I was open to new ideas. I knew something had to change, and if this guy said he could help me, then, okay, let's see what this is about.

From this moment forward, everything in my life would change. But I was still clueless.

The gentleman standing before me, offering

to help me, was Patrick Hayes, a retired forty-something-year-old, Wall Street professional, and a multi-millionaire. One of the first things that Patrick did was to lay in my hands a book: *Think and Grow Rich*, by Napoleon Hill. Patrick told me that if I did what he told me to do, and if I would allow him to mentor me through this book, he could help me get rich.

Game on! I was ready. And I certainly didn't realize then how *rich* I would become in every single area of my life through the study of this book and the still greater levels of awareness that came to me from beyond.

Now, you have to remember, I'm a high school dropout. Up until that moment in my life, I had held fast to the belief that I was dumb and stupid. I had never in my life read a book cover to cover. I knew how to read. I just didn't see any point in reading, because, after all, I couldn't learn. So why bother? When I saw the title, *Think and Grow Rich*, I was just about ready to quit then and there. In my mind, you had to be smart in order to think. And if you had to think in order to get rich, well, that took me right out of the equation from the get-go.

But, nonetheless, Patrick stuck with me. And slowly, step by step, he helped me see that my life up until that point was being controlled by the dominating thoughts and beliefs that I held about myself and my potential. He helped me see that I could change those thoughts; I could change those beliefs, and he would show me how to do that.

Patrick actually took me through *Think and Grow Rich,* line by line by line. He did not allow me to skip over a single word. And as he did this, I began to understand the power of establishing a burning desire within me, an all-consuming obsession for my life. Patrick helped me to overcome the fear of my past, the fear of my failings, the fear of my overwhelming limiting beliefs, and to establish a sense of faith in my own richness, in my own potential, and in my connection to the all-powerful source of my creation.

What I didn't realize until I was mentored through this book was that I had been using my imagination in entirely the wrong way. I had certainly been using my imagination to create my life, but all that I was creating was a life of chaos, anxiety, and disappointment. You see, I had been imagining all that I did *not* want—and as you imagine, so you create.

Patrick showed me the process of *making a decision* to do whatever it takes, that I would *persist* toward my dreams and desires, against all odds, all the while utilizing the gifts within me and the giftedness of those around me. I learned that I didn't have to know it all in order to accomplish great things. But I did have to tap into the greater consciousness of humanity, and of the source of humanity, and I had to open myself to receiving ideas that would be rejected by most people at first blush because of the apparent absurdity of such ideas.

I decided that, until Patrick proved to me in some way that he was either lying to me or that he was crazy, I would do anything and everything that he told me to do. I would do it in the exact manner in which he told me to do it. I would do it the number of times that he told me to do it. And I would keep doing it until he told me what to do next.

Since being mentored by Patrick, I have read *Think and Grow Rich* thousands of times. There are pieces of it that I know by memory, that I could recite to you at the drop of a hat. But knowledge doesn't change your life. It is the application of the knowledge that makes all the difference. As Patrick mentored me through *Think and Grow Rich* over the course of a few years, my life began to change. At first, the changes were subtle—the feeling tone of my life was the first thing to change. What I mean by this is that I began to notice a shift in my attitude, in my perspective, in my energy.

All in all, I began to feel more positive, more encouraged, and more hopeful for my future.

And then the physical manifestation of those changes began to show up in my life, especially in my finances. My business started to grow again. It was as if the invisible barrier that had been preventing my company from growing all of a sudden miraculously disappeared. In reality, the invisible boundaries of my own limiting beliefs and the voice of my ego-centered self-judgement were gradually diminishing in the amplitude and frequency of their vibration. In other words, this voice had been whispering to me all my life things like, "You're dumb and stupid," "You're just a high school dropout who will never amount to anything," "Who do you think you are to build a successful business? That will never happen," and so on and so forth. Now, as I studied and applied my new learning, these debilitating thoughts were becoming less frequent and less forceful and were being replaced by empowering thoughts that I could indeed achieve what I desired. And from this shift in my focus and my energy, I began creating results in my life that aligned with these new beliefs that I was forming within myself.

But let me make something very clear to you. I do not say this to be self-serving or to diminish in any way the work of Napoleon Hill, but Napoleon Hill himself never achieved great riches. At the end of his life, his relationships were close to destitute, and that *secret,* of which he speaks in the book, was one that he evidently was never able to live out fully. Now, the work of his life, the dedicated years of study and writing which he poured into *Think and Grow Rich* have changed thousands upon thousands of lives, tens of thousands, and probably even hundreds of thousands—of that much I am certain.

But, as Patrick pointed out to me, when you look on the cover of *Think and Grow Rich,* you will see printed on certain editions: "Over Ten Million Copies Sold." I do not think that ten million people have gotten rich from the reading and studying of *Think and Grow Rich.* But I did.

I did accomplish a level of financial achievement in my life which less than 0.05 percent of people in this world have ever achieved. And again, I don't say this to toot my own horn, because that is the *very last* thing that I would hope to communicate to you. Instead, what I seek to convey is that I took the teachings and the principles that Napoleon Hill laid out in *Think and Grow Rich,* and I applied them in my life, and I became financially wealthy. And if I can do it, a high school dropout who believed himself to be dumb and stupid for the first half of his life, so can you.

However—and here's the most important point of all—I realized that being financially wealthy would never equate to a complete richness in my life. And, as such, until I did certain things differently, there would always be an emptiness, a longing, and a certain unfulfilled void in my life. For, I had not created richness in my health. I had not created richness in my relationships. I had not created richness in my spiritual connection to my source. Even in my finances, I was still hitting a certain lid which I could not seem to surpass.

I knew something was missing. I knew that my handbook for achievement, which I had studied now for some years, had not given me all that I needed in order to create and experience the vastness of achievement and fulfilment that I believed was available to me in *all* areas of my life.

I began to dig deeper. And that digging led me within myself. And what I discovered was that there were three core principles, missing from the work of Napoleon Hill, that I would have to integrate into my very existence, and that I would have to adopt into the core of my being, if I was to move beyond mere financial success.

First of all, I realized I had to forgive. I had to forgive my mother for the abuse perpetrated upon my siblings and me. I learned that the bitterness and resentment festering in any area of one's life will always spill over into all other areas of life. So, I walked that difficult, painful, but freeing, path of forgiveness.

You, too, must engage in the process of true forgiveness, the process of releasing *them* to their highest good, and you to yours. When you carry bitterness within you, and you refuse to let it go, it will forever hold you back. I will vouch for this truth to the end of my days.

I also determined that, in order to live in the energy vortex of abundance, I needed to live on both sides of the equation. I could not merely receive. There is a give and a take, there is an ebb and a flow, there is a circulation to all things in life, and if I was only receiving, and missing the critical element of giving and of tithing, the movement of life with, in, and through me would be constricted and even halted altogether.

Despite the difficulty of entering into the true spirit of giving—not giving with regret, obligation, resentment, or score-keeping, but giving with the full expression of the abundance that is available to all of us—I have consistently followed through on this practice, and I have made it such a habit in my life that I cannot imagine my life without the practice of tithing. The rewards I have consequently reaped are immense and innumerable.

And finally, I learned that in the creation of everything, as I harness my inner capacity to produce that which I desire in my life, it must all be created in the energy of love in order for the fullness of that creation to be expressed. And it must be a love for all people, all things, all places, and even all states of being. I cannot simply *give* love to myself and others; I must *be* love. For love is indeed the highest energy frequency that exists in this universe. There is no greater power than love.

And so I invite you into this experiment, to study and live out the principles that Napoleon Hill teaches in *Think and Grow Rich* and to give careful consideration to the opportunity before you, to step beyond the mere pursuit of financial wealth, and to follow what I know will lead you to a much greater and fuller richness, encompassing all areas of your life.

As I was introduced to this journey of personal growth and the field of human potential, and as I walked this path, I knew that I needed to do for others as Patrick had done for me. He helped me open the eyes of my heart and of my mind in ways that I had never been able to do for myself. And as I opened up more and more to growth and transformation through the work of Napoleon Hill, these three principles continued to re-enter the field of vision that is my awareness.

Think and Grow Rich will always have a special place in my heart and will always be for me the first central teaching that brought me toward my truth. But were it not for these three spiritual principles that I have studied, adopted, and layered into the learning that I first gleaned from *Think and Grow Rich*, I would not be where I am today. And it is these three principles, of forgiveness, of tithing, and of love, that I truly believe have allowed me to shift from living a life of achievement to living a life of empowerment—from living a life focused on the building of myself and my own successes to expanding into the realm of multiplying success and abundance to others. And, in this way, I am able to experience riches in every realm of my life.

And if you, my dear reader, desire to be, to do, to have, to create more in your life, to leave a lasting impact in this world, to embolden and inspire in others the greatness that lies dormant within, you must understand these three principles.

You must embrace them, and you must embody them in everything you are and everything you do.

In the coming chapters, you will explore what I have explored and what I have applied in my life and have come to believe to be the critical elements to experience true richness in life. These three chapters have been written in the voice of Napoleon Hill, to resemble his writing style, in order to allow you to more easily integrate them with the teaching that you will also glean as you carry forward from the reading of this work to the study of the original text of *Think and Grow Rich*.

So, as I close this introduction, I bring to you the three missing chapters of *Think and Grow Rich*, the three missing keys to living a life of full abundance and true empowerment: forgiveness, tithing, and love.

FORGIVENESS

Chapter 2

THE meaning of the word "forgiveness" is, in simple language, "the action or process of letting go of anger or resentment."

While the riches, wealth, fame, and influence you seek may give you something of which you have not previously been in possession of, only FORGIVENESS can free you to truly enjoy what you seek. Forgiveness is perhaps the ultimate embodiment of the phrase "addition by subtraction."

Because of ignorance on the subject, the process of FORGIVENESS is often mistaken for simply letting a grievance go, like a breath that vanishes into the wind.

On the contrary, the beginning stage of forgiveness often starts with the act of leaning into the intensity of your anger. The desire for emotional expression is inborn and natural. Take away a toy from a baby, and you will see this to be true. The need to express or experience anger should not be submerged or eliminated. It should, in fact, be given ample release through forms of expression that enrich the soul.

Anger, like all emotions, is subject to the law of polarity. There are positive ways to express anger and there are negative ways. When you allow your anger to explode into a state of rage, losing control over your very demeanor, this is far from healthy or helpful in the process of ultimately releasing it. Instead of leading to healing and restoration, the outburst only causes harm to yourself and to others. This is one extreme of how anger can be expressed. In a similar manner, yet on the opposing end of the spectrum, when you suppress anger within yourself, and there is no acknowledgment or release of this emotion, you will spend much energy managing that bottled turmoil as you find small ways to express it through the planning and executing of passive-aggressive behavior upon others. Again, this prevents a healthy release that leads to healing. Though these are two apparent opposite examples of how anger is often expressed internally and externally, both lead to injury to oneself and to others and must only be characterized as negative.

The true polarity of these negative expressions of anger is found in moving yourself to a neutral state in how that anger is expressed. Rather than exploding into rage or bottling this emotion, you can use it to muster from within a healthy state of fiery self-empowerment. Your anger can be used as a catalyst to take a stand for yourself, recognizing that you deserve and are worthy of freedom from the inner and outer turmoil that will inevitably build in your life as this emotion remains within you. As you shift to this empowered state, you can then recognize that you do not need to allow yourself to be trodden upon like a figurative doormat, harboring much internal unrest; and in the same breath, you have the self-control within you to keep yourself from exploding in an over expression of emotion that breaks down human connection and destroys any semblance of calm in your life.

This is the true polarity of anger and the productive manner in which it must be utilized in the process of forgiveness.

It must be noted that THE STRENGTH OF YOUR ANGER IS IN DIRECT PROPORTION TO THE AMOUNT OF PAIN YOU FEEL INSIDE. Often, men and women are not even able to fully feel their own pain. This is not a weakness but rather a defense mechanism, put into place by divine design, in order to help human beings cope with their trauma. It is a short-term safety mechanism; yet, those who lack the self-awareness to realize this will eventually find that the very thing that helped them mitigate their initial pain will prevent them from ultimately letting it go.

In my Turning Point Retreat, I dedicate an entire session to this "letting go" process, which starts with the simple principle that a dream of the heart cannot grow in toxic soil. The soil of anger and resentment does not nurture and replenish, but rather suffocates and starves both the dream and the dreamer.

THE THREE PILLARS OF FORGIVENESS

The act of FORGIVENESS has three pillars whereby a person may re-establish oneself on sure footing. An important distinction to note is that all of these pillars must be *built*. They require action and, thus, all start with a verb. They are:

- Pillar 1: Recognize that you don't know the whole story
- Pillar 2: Learn to separate the being from the behavior

- Pillar 3: Ask for help in removing the poison of resentment

These pillars should be the focal point of what we aim to build, and during the process, we must be diligent to ensure no outside factor hinders their growth! Consider a physical pillar resting inside or outside a building. It can be weakened in a number of ways. It can be violently destroyed by a bulldozer, an explosion, or some extreme occurrence of Mother Nature. Other than the instances of demolition, wartime, or earthquake, pillars are generally not destroyed in a matter of seconds.

More common is the slow erosion of a pillar due to the elements of weather or neglect. A small crack can be the entry point for an outside agent that permeates the pillar and endangers the entire building from the inside out. It is the same with anger and resentment.

Upon visiting Greece and the Acropolis, I was amazed at the thought of its pillars withstanding centuries of war and the elements. BUILDING SOMETHING THAT STANDS THE TEST OF TIME REQUIRES TIME. The three pillars of forgiveness are the same. You will war with your old self, your strength and endurance tested. Just remember, for the last six thousand years of recorded history, all of the world's great teachers, religions, and spiritual practices have taught the principles contained in these three pillars as I have defined them.

No architect would draw plans to deliberately build a foundation upon weak soil. Similarly, it is vital that you diligently guard your emotions to keep your foundation strong. Little complaints and small grievances will accumulate and cultivate toxic emotions. This will spawn additional toxicity and eventually eat through a person's emotional well-being. Consider a married couple, two people who daily test one another's patience with small grievances. Small issues can balloon into explosive arguments or, worse, into harbored anger and resentment that go unspoken and unexpressed. Despite the intensity of the battle, there is yet a sliver of hope for reconciliation or progress as long as emotion is still in play. Truly, the most grievous sign that an intimate relationship is in danger is the WITHHOLDING OF LOVE. The absence of emotion or the intentional withholding of love is a clear sign that the second pillar has eroded significantly—the pillar of separating the being from the behavior. This is an example that we will explore in more depth in the pages to come, along with pillars one and three.

Think again of a dispute, of the emotions of hurt and pain experienced by both parties because they cannot see the truth that the other person is not comprised of their behavior, that their being is separate from the original or subsequent acts that caused the harm. When one cannot separate THE BEING FROM THE BEHAVIOR, as so often happens when an argument escalates, it is that inability to acknowledge this pillar of forgiveness that leads to the intentional act of withdrawing one's love.

Self-awareness is vital. For now, and the rest of your days, ample opportunities for small grievances will seek you out. These can derail not just your daily experiences, but actually take root in the soil of your heart for days to come. Whether this manifests through a person exhibiting rude behavior in a market, a hostile or negative conversationalist, or a motorist who drives recklessly, it is the HABIT OF TURNING SMALL SLIGHTS INTO LARGE GRIEVANCES that must be guarded against. Far too many people have done diligent, daily work in strengthening this most harmful habit!

To acquire true prosperity, you must cultivate different habits, which you will have ample opportunity to exercise—even daily. These habits are built upon the three aforementioned pillars, which we will now discuss.

PILLAR 1: RECOGNIZE THAT YOU DO NOT KNOW THE WHOLE STORY

This phase involves REMOVING THE DOMINATING THOUGHTS AND DESIRES for vengeance, retribution, punishment, getting even, or keeping score against people and allows empathy, understanding, compassion, and closure to take root instead. This often includes these key distinctions:

- You do not excuse the behavior to the degree that you allow yourself to be a doormat for the world, but you realize there may be reasons or circumstances behind it OF WHICH YOU ARE NOT AWARE.
- You recognize that there are always things you do not know, even about your own story.
- You start simple.
- You remember what it feels like to be judged.
- You acknowledge that to understand, you don't have to know the whole story.

Several years into my first business, I found myself at a crossroads. My business plateaued for two years, and I consulted a business mentor who, in turn, referred me to a Lutheran minister, Dr. Lee. Upon telling Dr. Lee my entrepreneurial challenges, I observed he did not write down a single note. I was noticeably upset at his apparent lack of interest but continued to tell him of my struggles for the next thirty minutes of our session. After I stopped telling my side of the story, Dr. Lee simply took his glasses off, looked me in the eye, and asked, "Paul, who do you need to forgive?"

Two things flashed into my mind. The first was that the good doctor must have had me confused with another client—I wasn't there seeking to give or gain forgiveness; I was there for business advice. The second was that I immediately knew what he was talking about.

He said, "Paul, you don't really think it is possible for a person to be stuck in one area of their life and not be stuck in every area of their life, do you? You don't really think that you're just stuck in your business, do you?" Dr. Lee said the blockage that was showing up in my business was really a blockage that was in my heart. He said, "Until you heal your heart, Paul, you're never going to be able to grow your business."

In my case, my childhood and adolescence were marked heavily by verbal, emotional, and physical abuse. The perpetrator was my own mother, and the trauma manifested itself in the form of a debilitating stutter, which drove me to even more embarrassment and shame. I will expound on this story in the next section, but for our purposes right now, the most important thing for me to acknowledge was that I did not know the whole story. I KNEW MY SIDE OF THE STORY AS THE VICTIM OF MY OWN MOTHER'S ABUSE.

As I followed Dr. Lee's instructions to practice forgiveness, I realized that my family history held the answers to a greater understanding of where my mother's own life trauma originated. Generations earlier, my grandparents set off from Calabria, Italy to the United States, where they started a family. They had an oldest son, a middle daughter, and a youngest son.

At that time, in an Italian family, girls were deemed almost worthless. Remember, this was the 1920s; as they say, it was a different time. It would have been absolutely appropriate for my grandfather or uncles to slap my mother's face at dinner, verbally berate her, or task her with all the chores of cleaning the table or doing laundry while the boys were free to play. I later discovered that my grandfather used to tie my mother to a chair to punish her, often leaving her in the cellar all day in the dark. Thus, the roots of her trauma were revealed. I did not know the whole story, her whole story. I only knew my version of the story.

This in no way justified my mother's behavior, but it did create an understanding of, and compassion for, how a woman who was raised in violence and trauma could perpetrate that same behavior on her own children, unless and until someone operating at a higher level of awareness could intervene.

A simple yet profound realization is found in THE ABILITY TO ACKNOWLEDGE THAT ANY GIVEN PERSON CAN ONLY DO THEIR BEST, TO THEIR LEVEL OF AWARENESS. This does not mean they do not know any better. My mother did know better. With every beating, every mean-spirited word, and every withholding of love, she knew that what she was doing was wrong. And yet, at the very same time, she lacked the awareness of how to live out that knowledge. She then did what we all do— she defaulted to old programming, even though it would produce results that she did not want.

Whenever a person behaves from a lower level of awareness, even though they have the intellectual knowledge that the behavior is wrong, it means they lack the awareness to act out and manifest that which they know. I would ask you: Are you aware of things in your life that you know you could do better, and yet you do not do those things?

How many of us know that exercise and healthy eating will lead to weight loss, and yet we don't do those things? How many of us know that stopping for two minutes every day and intentionally speaking words of love and encouragement to our children and loved ones would impact their lives in a positive way, and yet we don't do it? I have often taught in my lectures and workshops that the biggest gap in a person's life may very well be this knowing and doing gap. We know better; yet, we lack the awareness of how to export what we know.

In addition to having gathered knowledge and information during the course of your life, and having failed to export that which you know, consider this question: In just the last month, have you learned and become aware of something new about yourself that you didn't know before? Have you had a shift in your awareness that opened up a new knowing, a new understanding about yourself? (I would assume if you are reading this book, it is because you are on a journey of self-discovery, seeking greater awareness, and, as a result of your seeking, have likely found many new and empowering things about yourself.)

If the answer to this question is "yes," then it is not a great leap for you to deduce that you don't even know your own entire story—it's still being written. You and I and everyone else are works in progress, so how can you possibly know someone else's entire story? I created a statement for myself that helped me anchor this awareness, and I repeat it to myself whenever I find myself in a place of judgement against others: "If I were a block of marble, Michelangelo would still be chipping away at me!"

I love the visual of this power statement, as it reminds me that there is more to me than is revealed in my current results. I would encourage you, my dear reader, to use this power awareness statement, or to create your own, until the understanding of this pillar is deeply anchored in that powerful place: your subconscious mind.

The purpose of these questions is not to guilt you. It is to empower you to simply open the door. Acknowledging that you do not know yours—or anyone's—entire story gives you room to light a candle of compassion and understanding that can lead to forgiveness for yourself and others.

PILLAR 2: LEARN TO SEPARATE THE BEING FROM THE BEHAVIOR

The next pillar involves important phases one must acknowledge and embrace in order to move fully into FORGIVENESS:

1. Realize you may never forgive the act.
2. Realize you can still forgive the perpetrator.
3. Realize that when you move beyond the act, healing can begin.

The greatest forces are "intangible", and yet, when it comes to FORGIVENESS (or the lack thereof), the effects are clearly tangible. To some degree, every person will carry consequences based on the actions and offenses of others. *FORGIVENESS does not equate to a justification of those actions.*

THE GREATEST CHALLENGE I FACED when learning to practice forgiveness was the trauma I experienced as a child. There were many occasions when, as a third grader, I went to school with black eyes as a result of my mother's blows. Oftentimes my siblings and I would be pulled out of bed by our hair and thrown onto the porch in the single-digit Pittsburgh winter—simply because she was convinced one of us had hidden her silver comb. The panic and anxiety from even hearing my mother march up the stairs to my room resulted in my development of a stutter, which led me to more shame and embarrassment through my adolescence. Very few people develop a stutter because of neurological reasons; it is usually based on an emotional trauma.

As time passed, my mother was steeped in complete denial that she ever did anything wrong. The anger and resentment took deep root in me, and I purposely refrained from sending her Mother's Day or birthday cards after turning the age of sixteen. One year, I told her that I planned to attend Easter lunch at her home and then waited until one o'clock in the afternoon to tell her I would not be coming. This was all in an effort to hurt her, to get even.

The abuse of a child (or anyone) is never justifiable, and yet, when we experience trauma, we are prone to believe the trauma was not as bad as it seems. We tell ourselves that this is normal, and we numbly accept it as the way life must be. This is a defense mechanism.

Conversely, when the rush of anger and resentment finally reveals itself, we swing the pendulum equally to the other extreme. We are blinded by anger and we LOSE THE ABILITY TO SEPARATE THE PERSON (THE BEING) FROM THE DEED (THE BEHAVIOR). This, too, is a defense mechanism. It is temporarily useful while one remains in an environment of abuse, as it is less painful to feel the anger and the resentment instead of the helplessness and hopelessness, but in the end, it prevents us from forgiving the person. In the absence of the very empathy that we look for in order to heal ourselves, we withhold empathy from the perpetrator or try to hurt the person with the same intensity with which we were hurt.

You may not have undergone this level of abuse, or you may have experienced worse. I could go on in more painful detail about the abuses perpetrated on my siblings and me by our mother, but doing so would accomplish nothing more for you, the reader, and could act as a negative trigger for many who also suffered from abuse as a child.

What is of most importance is the realization that the decision now remains with you. Life is after all a "you and you" deal when it comes to taking responsibility for your own life. A simple start to separating the being from the behavior is to remove the words "always" and "never" from your vocabulary. My mother didn't always beat us. It would not be accurate to say she never showed us love. The removal of the words ALWAYS and NEVER creates space for a new and healthier narrative. By removing these absolutes, always and never, in the forgiveness process, we can begin to align ourselves with the law of impermanence and release the attachments we have created to our version of our life's story. A person cannot always breathe in; they must breathe out. A person cannot always work; they must also rest. My mother wasn't always mean and unloving; at times, she was loving and kind. With this understanding and release of the absolutes, I could then begin to harvest the good within her. This leads us to the next pillar.

PILLAR 3: ASK FOR HELP IN REMOVING THE POISON OF RESENTMENT

The road to FORGIVENESS is rarely a journey walked alone. Trusted friends and confidants are often vital in aiding you to experience freedom in this area, and oftentimes people also look to a higher power for help.

Lest I be misunderstood, I wish to state that this last pillar is not established simply by asking for help. It requires forethought and intentional action, often entailing:

- Techniques such as meditation, writing letters, and visualization
- The intention to forgive fully and not half-heartedly

- A shift in perspective and a daily practice of asking, "Who should I forgive?"

These practices are exactly that: practices. Through intentional repetition, they strengthen your ability to process pain and open your heart. It is better to live with a hurting heart than a closed one. A contracted and closed heart is like a straitjacket on your soul; it renders you unable to move.

Ritual is a powerful aid in opening your heart during these times of pain and contraction. A life devoid of ritual is flat and lacks rhythm and texture. Human beings are creatures of habit, and rituals help create new habits. VISUALIZATION AND MEDITATION are core practices for most, if not all, top performers across nearly every industry. Other chapters in this book have outlined the power of visualizing the money, access, or influence you seek. In this vein, you must VISUALIZE YOURSELF BEING FREE OF ANGER AND RESENTMENT.

Yet another powerful ritual is found in the written word. It has been said that THOUGHTS DISENTANGLE THROUGH THE LIPS AND THE FINGERTIPS. Writing a letter to the perpetrator is a powerful ritual that can open your heart so that healing can come. Sending this letter is not always advisable, nor is it even possible at times. If the person who has wronged you is no longer alive, write the letter and cast it into the sea (there is biodegradable paper for this) or burn it. If re-engaging the individual would only stir up waters better left undisturbed, again, cast it into the sea or burn it. If you perform this ritual truthfully, you will move toward FORGIVENESS more readily than the majority of people. As stated above, forgiveness is always a deal between you and yourself. It does not involve the other person, and so you do not need the other person in order to move forward in forgiveness.

The power of ritual allows you to face your pain and grief through a process. When facing anger, bitterness, or resentment, the question one must ask is, "Is this mine to carry?"

Is it your highest calling, bestowed upon you by the universe and the divine, to carry this burden? If it is not, and it rarely ever is, then we must give to our God that which is his to carry. Saying a simple prayer daily, and every time these old hurts rise to the surface of your awareness, can and will release you of this burden. One ritual that I have found helpful has been to say these words with deep sincerity and a willingness to let this burden go, to pick up my own mat and go on in my life:

"Father, I choose now to release (this person or this situation) to their highest good and me to mine. I now give (this person or this situation) to you, knowing that holding on does not serve me and keeps me from expressing all of the potential you have given me. I recognize, as a creative being with dominion over all things, that I am fully resourced and empowered to release (this person or this situation) now and for eternity in the full awareness that this is not mine to carry. Thank you, Father. It is so."

Burdens of any kind will weigh you down on your journey to whatever you seek, but resentment and unforgiveness in particular will grind your pursuit to a halt. Oftentimes, resentment manifests in bizarre ways. One such story is as follows.

THE SICK CYCLE OF RESENTMENT, RESISTANCE, REVENGE

Early in my entrepreneurial days, I fell into the sick-cycle carousel of RESENTMENT, RESISTANCE, and REVENGE, nearly crippling my future success. This was not even predicated on a particular person doing harm directly to me.

I was ecstatic the first year I made two hundred and fifty thousand dollars, until I had to confer with my accountant regarding taxes. I understood the need to pay more tax, but unbeknownst to me was the fact that, in addition to the dollar increase, the overall percentage off my income would increase as well. Business math was new to me, and I did not realize that this was the government's way of "the more you make, the more we take."

As incredibly foolish and small-minded as it sounds, the following year I WATCHED MY INCOME AND PACED MYSELF SO I WOULD MAKE LESS THAN two hundred and fifty thousand dollars. I was restricting and withholding my God-given skill, talent, and ability to grow my business simply out of RESENTMENT toward the government and their usurious tax plan. I was going to teach them a lesson.

Once resentment set in, my self-limiting plan required a twisted sense of discipline to keep my income under that threshold. I exhibited a stunning display of RESISTANCE to new deals, new promotions, and new ideas that could have far exceeded my previous year's income. All of this was to enact REVENGE on the government, as if I were significant enough to hurt them anyway.

As petty as my attitude in this story was, the point is this: When we are driven by

RESENTMENT, we become blind and delusional in our reasoning. We become like the proverbial bull who only sees red. This is a sick-cycle carousel, and the only way to break a cycle or stop the carousel is to get off the ride.

Nature has bestowed upon humankind absolute control over but one thing: THE FREE WILL OF OUR THOUGHT. Thus, there lies a great power in the space between stimulus and our response. Within the space between stimulus and response is the power to choose our attitude. Upon an offense, you may not be able to control your visceral emotion to it; yet, the attitude thereafter can be controlled.

Many people walk through life looking for a reason to be offended. It fuels them, yet they do not understand that RESENTMENT IS AN ENERGY THAT, BY LAW, MUST EXPRESS ITSELF AND EXPAND. Resentment expresses and expands into resistance and revenge. The purpose of REVENGE is to cause the other person to feel the pain that we believe they caused, and we relegate our life's purpose to keeping score. Observe any kind of game or match and you will see that the most successful and focused players are playing the game, not keeping score.

THE FOUR STAGES OF FORGIVENESS

The purpose of this section is to turn the spotlight of attention upon the process of forgiveness. You can fully commit to every other principle outlined in this book, but if you neglect FORGIVENESS, you will never step into the full-potentiated self. Here, then, is the place to give yourself the opportunity to determine how much of the philosophy of FORGIVENESS you have absorbed.

There can be no compromise between RESENTMENT and the FULL-POTENTIATED SELF! The two are in direct conflict with one another. There are four basic stages of forgiveness, some combination of which all humans move through at one time or another. The process is not always followed in this order, and it differs from person to person.

In the **FIRST STAGE**, you are ANGRY. You justify your anger because you have been wounded and wronged. The tendency here is to look to another person's action rather than your reaction. Blame is common at this stage, and you are yet unable to separate the being from the behavior.

In the **SECOND STAGE**, you realize that the hurt and anger are not serving you positively and that these are, in fact, likely affecting other areas of your emotional and day-to-day life negatively. At this point, you take actions to move forward and start to see the other side of the story. Perhaps you simply decide it is time to let it go. At the end of this stage, you are no longer pained or upset, and you feel you have forgiven the person—even if that person is yourself.

In the **THIRD STAGE**, you have experienced the positive results of letting go. You become better able to let new grievances go quickly and more consciously. You make the decision to forgive more quickly because you see how well that serves you in your life. You realize that to be the person you want to be, forgiveness must be a part of your life. You may even consciously vow to not let anger or pain consume you ever again.

In the Third Stage, you are keenly aware that the duration of your anger and pain is entirely up to you. You are in control, and you know it. You may practice letting go and forgiving in situations that linger from before you made it to this stage. You find it easier to forgive, regardless of what the pain or harm has been.

In the **FOURTH STAGE**, you are able to choose to not take offense or be angered or pained in the first place. You are, in effect, ready to forgive even before you feel the feelings of which you would have needed to let go in the past. You are not reactive when it comes to triggers, whether significant or minor. The Fourth Stage is marked by at least some of these realizations:

- I refuse to waste time or energy on the discomfort caused by anger or hurt.

- I am able to forgive myself, forgive others, forgive life, and forgive God.

- I know how it hurts when people don't forgive me.

- Unless I let go and forgive, I am stuck. If I am stuck in anger and pain, I am unable to fully appreciate the beauty and goodness of life.

- Taking personal offense isn't often an accurate reaction. People operate out of self-interest, and someone else's self-interest does not necessarily fit with mine.

Considerable courage is required to move through these stages, and they are not always followed in order in all situations. You may feel such strong positive feelings for some people that you go directly to Stage Four. There are times when your pain is so deep and raw that you stay in Stage

One for months or years. Reader, beware!

FORGIVING YOURSELF

A majority of this chapter has dealt with forgiveness toward others, but what about forgiving ourselves? Forgiving yourself involves the same pillars and practices outlined in this chapter. My teaching and business partner, Roddy Galbraith, says, "FORGIVING YOURSELF SHIFTS YOUR ENERGY FROM PAIN TO POWER."

Oftentimes, it is helpful to walk through this process of forgiving yourself with another person because of the outside perspective they provide you. Have you ever spoken with a friend or colleague regarding a topic in your past and realized, through the course of the conversation, some memory or insight you had dismissed or forgotten? It is possible that you have never even known the whole story behind yourself.

Regardless of what you have done, realize that your act was only in direct proportion to the level of your own awareness. You may have known better, but you were not able to express and manifest that knowledge in a better way. You are better now, and you are continuing to grow into your full-potentiated self.

The ritual of writing a letter to yourself, or

to create a healthy outlet to talk through your pain and resentment, can be incredibly healing. In order to forgive, it is imperative to stop identifying yourself with the suffering that was caused, especially if you were the cause. Until one truly learns to forgive, one can never expect to truly be rich.

FORGIVENESS IS A GIFT YOU GIVE TO YOURSELF.

IT IS FROM YOU, FOR YOU, BY YOU.

TITHING

Chapter 3

I remind the reader that the purpose of this chapter is to help you organize and apply the knowledge herein and convert it into a benefit for what you seek. I make these remarks because whenever the concept of TITHING is discussed, the majority of people feel there is an ulterior motive on the part of whoever is advocating the practice.

Keep in mind, I am no religious leader and seek to derive no benefit from any donation or gift you render. This is solely for your benefit. The practice of TITHING can change your financial destiny. The concepts here should not only be studied and digested, they should be *acted upon*. Remember that riches start with a state of mind and with a definiteness of purpose. You must acquire the state of mind that will attract riches, and perhaps the most important state of mind you can attain is a mind that is set on GENEROSITY, PROSPERITY, CONSCIOUSNESS, and ABUNDANCE.

A TITHE, by definition, is a measurement of one tenth of something. The PRACTICE OF TITHING is the giving away of ten percent of your time, talent, or treasure (money); the combination of these three is what I call your life force. Tithing is an essential practice in attracting a greater flow of abundance in your life *through the counterintuitive discipline of giving it away*. It thereby makes you the causative force in the law of reciprocity. Tithing is often misunderstood as a tax, debt, obligation, or remittance of payment, particularly to a religious institution. At the core, tithing is actually an act that serves as a vehicle by which you attain AWARENESS. This awareness is not of self, but rather an awareness of your connectedness to the source of all supply: God. It is an awareness that your wealth, means, possessions, and influence stem from this Infinite Source. When properly done, tithing attracts more than financial wealth; it results in spiritual wholeness and integration.

Most of us, at some time in our life, for many different reasons, become disconnected from the AWARENESS of our oneness with this Infinite Source. We develop a learning model that causes us to operate from our conditions and circumstances in our physical world, and we fail to see that those conditions are far more limited than our potential and who we are as spiritual beings. Tithing PUTS YOU BACK INTO CONSCIOUS CONNECTION TO THE SOURCE so you can create your highest good and step into your full-potentiated self, rather than living from current circumstances. The goal is for YOU TO LIVE FROM SOURCE AND NOT FROM THE CONDITIONS OR CIRCUMSTANCES OR RESOURCES IN YOUR LIFE, whether they be plentiful or seemingly restricted.

If we speak strictly in monetary terms, I would ask the reader: What would it profit your soul to possess great wealth, only to be plagued each day by the insatiable and soul-sucking affliction called GREED? What would it profit your soul to have everything you desire, only to see and interact with the world through the lens of AN UNGIVING HEART? This kind of person will ultimately possess exactly what their beliefs and actions warrant: a barren life devoid of dear friends, unconditional love, inner joy, and true riches.

Resistance to the principle of tithing is to be expected and is common in the beginning. Objections will include, among others, the idea that the practice is outdated, unsubstantiated, superstitious, religious, foolhardy, or just too difficult to do. Some may see my advocacy of tithing to be self-serving, nothing more than a cosmic "give to get" scheme. Nothing could be further from the truth! A closer examination of these objections reveals a heart mired in scarcity and lack and, in fact, is in direct contradiction to the principles outlined in this book.

Many people make the mistake of diverting considerable amounts of creative energy to worry. Questions bombard them. "Where will my next resource come from? When will the next breakthrough come? How will I ever have enough?" Note that *none of these questions serve as fertile soil for new ideas, fresh creativity, and inspired insights*. They serve no purpose but to keep you from your full-potentiated self! They serve only to rob you of the abundant, unrestricted life by keeping you focused on current, or even imaginary, negative circumstances!

YOUR CURRENT PHYSICAL CIRCUMSTANCES WILL NEVER DICTATE WHAT YOU CAN CREATE AS A LIFE BEYOND WHAT YOU HAVE. Bathe in the wisdom of that statement! Read it aloud, then read it again and again! Your physical circumstances will never tell you that your life can be richer and more abundant than it is right now. The creativity, imagination, connections, and solutions you seek are not found in your current circumstances any more than water is found on a random dune in the Sahara Desert! They are found by tapping into and staying in alignment with the vibration of abundance and blessing that comes from your SOURCE, with tithing being the tuning mechanism.

THE FIVE PRINCIPLES OF TITHING

I invite you to open your heart to these five principles. When objections rise up, take closer examination upon yourself to find the root from which they stem. Is the soil of your heart rich and fertile? Or is it rocky, hard, and anchored in lack, scarcity, and limitation, to such an extent that it would yield no fruit, no matter how much seed, sun, and water is given it? Search your heart, dear friend! MOST PEOPLE HAVE UPHILL DREAMS BUT DOWNHILL HABITS. Tithing is the ultimate habit that brings breakthrough. Now, the five principles of tithing are:

1. Start where you are.
2. Give ten percent, because that is what "tithe" means.
3. Give immediately.
4. Give to an institution that practices God's law, or to where you feel God is leading you to give. Sometimes this

can and will be to an individual who doesn't need money. Remember, tithing is not about money; it is about connection.
5. Give quietly and privately.

START WITH WHERE YOU ARE.

While the goal is to give ten percent, some people will be in situations where that amount is simply not feasible. If giving a tithe renders you unable to pay for the basic needs for you and your family, do not start with ten percent, and do not start with money.

Be truthful! Many a person will say they simply cannot give ten percent, citing that they have no disposable income and can barely pay for necessities. Upon closer inspection, however, it is apparent that their definition of necessities includes all manner of special amenities, including the latest modern appliances, entertainment services, and luxuries. Cable television, two-hundred-dollar bottles of wine, and a housemaid do not qualify as necessities! If you are truthfully in a situation that precludes you from giving ten percent, then start with two percent, or tithe your time. The key differentiation is this: YOU ARE NOT WAITING FOR CONDITIONS AND CIRCUMSTANCES IN YOUR LIFE TO CHANGE. Rather, you are the one dictating the change. You are becoming the causative force in your life.

The important thing is to start and to *give by percentage*. WHEN YOU GIVE BY PERCENTAGE, WHATEVER THAT PERCENTAGE IS, YOU TAKE YOUR GIVING OUT OF THE EMOTIONAL REALM. Your emotions are powerful, and they will nearly always lead you to operate out of fear and scarcity. Neglect to keep them in check and they will cause your giving to fall prey to judgment and subjectivity.

WHY, PRAY TELL, IS IT TEN PERCENT?

In my experience, ten percent seems to be the perfect amount that keeps you on an edge; THE PERFECT AMOUNT TO SHIFT YOUR FOCUS FROM GETTING TO GIVING. Historical documents show that tithing was a widespread practice in the Ancient Middle East, and most people are familiar with the tithe as a foundational teaching in both Judaism and Christianity. However, many a successful man or woman, of no particular religious faith, have stated the peculiar power in the giving of ten percent. It seems that ten percent is the perfect amount to create that balance in our lives. Initially, giving ten percent may be met with negative focus. The goal is to release that negative energy so that connectedness with the Source can occupy its space. The practice develops a spirit of trust between you and God. This is you trusting that God will provide beyond what you see and experience in your physical world.

Resistance often manifests in seemingly innocuous questions, which include, but are not limited to, "Do I give of my gross or my net income? Why or why not? When should I give? Do I need to give retroactively, as if I have accumulated a great debt that now must be paid to the universe?" The idea of tithing can be so distasteful that people will mire themselves in debate, petty questions, and so forth, all in an effort to actually prevent themselves from doing that which ushers in transformation, which is the simple act of GIVING. The same energy expended to resist the tithe would be better used as a catalyst for ideas and creativity on how to increase your own supply, would it not?

I have asked all these questions and more, and my conclusion now is this: SUSPEND YOUR QUESTIONS AND JUDGMENT AND, INSTEAD, OPEN YOURSELF TO THE AWARENESS THE PRINCIPLE HAS TO OFFER. There is ancient wisdom in this principle. Imagine taking on a business partner who agrees to take only ten percent while affording you limitless imagination and creativity and access to greater influence. Would you not do it?

IF YOU WANT MORE INCREASE, YOU MUST GIVE MORE INCREASE.

You ATTRACT what you want more of in your life by BECOMING what you want more of! If a person wants more friends, she becomes more friendly. If a person craves more love, he becomes more loving. Isn't it odd then, that when we desire financial increase, we tend to do the exact opposite? We close our wallets, our hands, and ultimately our heart, convinced that the act of WITHHOLDING our resources will actually lead to an increase of them. Instead of drawing as if from the flow of a fresh river or the vastness of an ocean, we construct protective barriers around our supply, not realizing we have created a pond where no new life can flow in or out.

I was able to spend some time in Israel, and I had the opportunity to visit the Dead Sea. It is a fascinating place to be. No living vegetation or sea animals can exist in the Dead Sea. The salinity of its water is what prevents life from growing and flourishing. And the reason it is DEAD is because there is no outflow. Water feeds this sea from the Jordan River, but the Sea does not give. It is a place of restriction. Life cannot exist in a state of restriction. I realized when I was there, and I saw it with my own eyes, that the same is true for men and women. When we restrict ourselves, when we restrict the flow of resources and abundance through us and out to others, the RESTRICTION is a death sentence to our growth.

Are your thoughts, beliefs, and actions in true alignment with the outcome that you DESIRE? If you want more increase, are you becoming a person of increase? The proverb was not "Get and then give" but rather, "Give and then it will be given unto you in full measure." Yes, I have warred with my own soul and with God about the tithe! My ego (which some have said stands for "Edging God Out") would often say things like, "The tenant paid me a thousand dollars but the mortgage on the house is eight hundred, so I'm really only making two hundred dollars. Shouldn't I just tithe from the two hundred?" Or, in another instance: "I received a three-thousand-dollar tax rebate but tithed on the original money, so isn't God double dipping?" My own words convicted me, for I saw it as an obligation, or worse, a punishment! The phrase, "have to tithe" is a greater reflection of the posture of my heart than it is of the number on my bank statement!

In light of this, I have personally adopted the practice of giving on any and all monies received, whether tax refunds, rents, retirement, social security, and so forth. Such a posture allows me to LEVERAGE THE POWER OF TITHING IN MY GOAL SETTING. Consider what would happen if you POSITIONED YOURSELF FOR INTENTIONAL ABUNDANCE, factoring in the tithe to shape your goals and subsequent actions? Tithing allows your desires to become a vibrational match with the source of all supply, providing you the imagination, opportunity, and attraction of all you need to attain your desired outcomes. I purport this to be a real, physical, universal law, not just a spiritual principle.

GIVE IMMEDIATELY

As soon as you receive, give. Any businessman or businesswoman will feel the temptation to negotiate the terms of this line item. The argument will often sound as such: "I secured a payment of ten thousand dollars from a client, but the duration of the contract is for three months. Wouldn't it be prudent to hold on to this money, or at least part of it, in case I have a shortfall next month? There are utilities to pay. We have overhead costs, and I can give the tithe at the end of the next quarter."

The ego says, "I'll give when I'm good and ready." No, the practice is to immediately give the tithe. Do not disconnect the giving from the receiving. Furthermore, the practice of giving immediately cuts off and eliminates "rainy day" syndrome. IF YOU PLAN FOR A RAINY DAY, YOU WILL GET ONE. IF YOU SAVE IN CASE OF A SHORTFALL, YOU WILL CREATE ONE.

Lest I be misunderstood, there is no wrong to be found in saving. Rather, we must THINK ACCURATELY. Would you, in absolute truth, diligently save that ten percent, or would you spend it? Recall that there is NO HOPE for the person who is dishonest by choice. Sooner or later, your deeds will catch up to you. You must be on diligent guard against thinking from a place of lack and limitation; otherwise, that is what you will attract and create!

Lastly, the money is not yours! You are the steward of God's money, and it is for His work in the world through you. This is a vital level of awareness from which to operate, for it is the source of your connection. You are doing God's work in the world, acting as his servant here on earth!

GIVE TO AN INSTITUTION THAT PRACTICES GOD'S LAW OR WHERE GOD LEADS YOU TO GIVE

The origins of tithing are rooted in giving to a spiritually minded group that is teaching

God's law. Most often this is going to be a religious house, though the application of this practice will differ according to each person. My recommendation for you is to tithe to the house even if you are rarely, or never, in attendance there. If you know they do God's work, support them without judgment. If you don't belong to a religious house, give to charities and philanthropies you deem important. There is no shortage of organizations that are doing great work and would be worthy places for you to give. A wonderful organization that serves children in need is the Eliza Mae Foundation, one to which you may give knowing that your tithe is directly impacting the lives of vulnerable children who need this support in order to develop and thrive in their own lives. *(www.elizamae.org)*

As you grow in the practice of tithing, the door to DEVELOPING YOUR INTUITION presents itself. Because of your connectedness to God, you become a conduit of resource for others. Expect moments when you feel guided to give to a certain individual, and not even because they are in financial need. To think this is about charity is to miss the point.

At times, I have felt led to support an individual who I know would put the money toward growing a business, providing jobs to a community, and helping more people. Other times, I have been led to give to a family with a note that simply says, "I was guided to send this to you. If you prayed ever in your life for a financial blessing, it's just been answered." Regardless of where I am led to give, I give *without* asking God, "Are you sure?" The power in the tithe is that the money has already been set apart to give away.

GIVE QUIETLY

Refrain from talking about your sacrifice, or the blessing. The only time you should speak of such matters is to help another begin the practice, or to support, encourage, and bear good witness to people who are in the practice already or in serious consideration of it. This is not occasion to lament to your colleagues and friends that you cannot purchase something because you gave the money away. Conversely, do not make a spectacle of your giving. There are times when you will not be able to help receiving publicity for your gifts. Charities often highlight key donors, or there may be instances where you publicly discuss your gift in order to raise awareness for that said cause. In general practice, however, this is a private matter between you and God and should never be done to feed your own ego.

The importance is in understanding that you RECOGNIZE THAT YOUR TITHE DID

NOT COME FROM YOU—IT HAS COME THROUGH YOU. See yourself as a conduit and channel through which God is expressed. The practice of tithing will allow you to live in the full awareness of your oneness with God. When led to give quietly to an individual, use the occasion to encourage that person. "This is from God, through me, to you. Isn't it wonderful that you and I were brought together in this unique moment in time and space? I am honored to give this to you but please understand, this is not from me. This is from God, through me." Such small, yet meaningful, words can open another's heart to a perspective of abundance and to an awareness of God working in their life.

THE SHIFT TO ABUNDANCE AND GENEROSITY

My journey is similar to many of the people featured in this book. I had no exceptional qualities, natural talent, or connections beyond those of the average person, nor did I have any kind of financial inheritance by which to get started. I came from humble beginnings but dutifully applied the principles of Napoleon Hill's original text and these three missing, yet powerful, principles, making them my own. As I did, wealth and opportunities found me, so much so that I OFTEN WONDERED WHERE THEY HAD BEEN HIDING ALL

THOSE LEAN YEARS BEFORE I HAD THIS NEW AWARENESS.

To look at the tithe strictly through a financial lens is a mistake. Giving a hundred dollars on one thousand dollars might seem difficult, but it is much easier emotionally in the beginning than giving one thousand dollars on ten thousand. When I surpassed the one-million-dollar income level for the first time, I will readily admit it was emotionally difficult to tithe a hundred thousand dollars. People may say to a millionaire, "It's easy for you to give ten percent, you make a million dollars!" The dollar amount of the tithe is greater, but that doesn't mean it becomes easier to give. Remember, I said that ten percent is the perfect amount to keep you on that edge of trusting God, the Source of all supply. With greater amounts, there is, in fact, more temptation to withhold the tithe because of what can be done with that degree of money, be it to pay off loans, purchase a home, or put it toward retirement.

In one instance, I was speaking with a client about business practices and soon felt my ego step in and my pride well up. I told him my tactics on maximizing credit card, airline, and hotel points and that, as a result of these tactics, I had accumulated millions of points. I was very proud of myself, and my ego was at full boil. As I lay my head on the pillow that evening, I felt God say, "Where are my points? Don't I get ten percent of your airline, credit card, and hotel points?" Rebellion ensued. "I already tithed on that money. These are *my* points!" It was soon after that I conceded that these companies have programs whereby you can donate points to charity. And *my* points were never *my* points; I was simply the custodian of those points and was given ninety percent of them for serving as that custodian!

The issue is not about whether tithing is hard or easy. This is about a SHIFT IN YOUR PERCEPTION and your continual awareness of your connectedness to the Source. As you acquire riches and abundance, you will face the temptation to cease the practice of tithing. It will be a great temptation. You will reason with the universe, feel the pull to take control, and rationalize your decision by saying, "I need to hold onto this for my security."

Ten percent really is the perfectly ordained amount to keep you on the edge of FAITH versus SECURITY. The majority of people look to money for security. This is a myth. You must accept that you will never have security. Peace, yes. Security, no. Tithing brings you to a place of peace, for it draws you into communication with God, who gives you security. You cannot be a tither and not be connected to God every single day.

TITHING WAS THE VEHICLE TO FINDING MY RELATIONSHIP WITH GOD. As a businessman, and because of my childhood upbringing that caused me not to trust God, God did not stand a chance at getting into my heart. He had to go through my wallet. People who don't know me envy me because of the "break" they feel life yielded me. They see me in the days of triumph, without taking the trouble to investigate the *cause* of my success. The cause was God; my responsibility was to stay connected to God through tithing.

As outlined in an earlier chapter, I was a traumatized child. My future was bleak, and I believed life was lived by default and not by design. With two hundred dollars and a used vacuum cleaner, I started a cleaning business in my early twenties. Any money I made early in my life was a result of scrappy, hard work. As I saw increase come into my life, each level brought with it the same challenge to grow in my generosity. As I grew in the practice of tithing, I felt led to tithe beyond my treasure. IT IS NOT UNCOMMON TO TITHE FROM YOUR TIME AND TALENT ON TOP OF WHAT YOU GIVE FINANCIALLY.

A GREATER PURPOSE THAN JUST MONEY

At some point, acquiring more wealth will not be as fulfilling as it once was, and setting financial goals will not generate as much excitement or passion. The threshold at which this happens may differ from person to person, but the phenomenon remains the same. What is to become of life once a person's home is paid off, substantial savings are in the bank, and investments bring in regular cash flow? Do we just eat, drink, and be merry until death calls us home? John Maxwell said, "Once you've tasted significance, success is never enough. You can never attain significance financially." No amount of money alone is enough to make you feel truly significant, yet it is possible to make twenty-five thousand dollars a year, give two thousand and five hundred dollars to a worthy cause, and feel as significant as Mother Teresa.

While attaining wealth for yourself and your loved ones is a noble desire, there is a newfound joy in using your KNOWLEDGE ON HOW TO GENERATE WEALTH and the TITHE to contribute to others. Personally, my excitement and creativity flow much more freely at the idea of making a million dollars so I can send a hundred thousand dollars to, say, a school in need.

One of my business partners, Roddy Galbraith, and I have funded water systems and schools and have purchased much-needed equipment or transportation for causes we care about. Seeing need sparks inspiration for how we can generate money to give away. There are actually times we have decided to launch and sell a product with the revenue goal of five hundred thousand dollars in order to be able to give fifty thousand dollars away. One such cause is Paraguayan music teacher, Favio Chavez, and his Recycled Orchestra of Cateura, a children's orchestra in Paraguay that performs with materials recycled from a trash landfill near Asuncion. The group, featured in the stellar documentary *The Landfill Harmonic*, has played with the New York Philharmonic and the Boston Pops, among others, all with instruments recycled from trash. We were able to give them a bus for their travels.

Setting a goal to give—does this not align with the six, definite, practical steps outlined in Hill's original text?

- First, fix in your mind the exact amount of money you desire.
- Second, determine exactly what you intend to give in return for the money you desire.

- Third, establish a definite date when you intend to possess the money you desire.
- Fourth, create a definite plan for carrying out your desire, and begin at once.
- Fifth, write out a clear, concise statement of the answers to the previous four steps.
- Sixth, read your written statement aloud, twice daily, and as you read— see and feel and believe yourself already in possession of the money.

Every human being who reaches the age of understanding of the purpose of money wishes for it. Many people will say, "Money just doesn't matter to me." This is their prerogative, but what should matter is what money can do. Money can do much good in the world. If you set your goals based on the amount of money you want to tithe, you will see your abundance ENTRUSTED to you. You will succeed because you choose a definite goal, place all your energy, all your willpower, all your effort, and everything else to back that goal.

We who desire to accumulate riches should remember the real leaders of the world always have been men and women who harnessed, and put into practical use, the intangible, unseen forces of unborn opportunity and have converted those forces into cities, jobs, charities, technology, and every form of convenience that makes life more pleasant. This changed world requires practical dreamers who can and will put their dreams into action. The practical dreamers have always been, and always will be, the patternmakers of civilization. The oak sleeps in the acorn. The bird waits in the egg. And in the tithe, untold abundance stirs. THIS WORLD NEEDS YOU RICH.

LOVE

Chapter 4

The definition of a wealthy life simply cannot be confined to numbers on a bank account statement or a list of assets. The quest to grow rich is not one of merely acquiring material wealth. Rather, it is a quest to live from a place inside the soul that is more awake, more alive, and more aware. LOVE IS THE HIGHEST FREQUENCY IN THE UNIVERSE, and it is in love that we are made complete. LOVE DISSOLVES ALL SEPARATION!

If we truly seek to become our highest full-potentiated self, we must be in alignment with the frequency and vibration that is most in harmony with any person's highest full-potentiated self, and that is the frequency and vibration of love. Love is the frequency that expands the boundlessness of the entire universe; it is the frequency of

Infinite Intelligence, and it is the language, purpose, and essence of God, the Grand Overall Designer of all things in the universe. Time and again in this book, we have explored the notion that our THOUGHTS can bring forth the energy we need in order to manifest our desires. We, like our Creator, are born to be and act as creators.

In the same way that the human mind responds to stimuli that leads to enthusiasm, creative imagination, and so forth, the universe likewise responds to stimuli. When we live in alignment with love, we are in tune with the highest frequency that exists. I have said already, "Love is the highest frequency in the universe." You may ask what this means.

THE PERFECT UNI-VERSE: ONE

Are you aware that there is scientific evidence that we exist in a perfectly organized and balanced universe? It is a UNI-verse: one presence, one power, one life. I bring to mind the work of Dr. Michael Turner, the widely quoted astrophysicist at the University of Chicago and America's premier physics laboratory, Fermilab. He describes the fine-tuning of the universe this way: "The precision is as if one could throw a dart across the entire universe and hit a bullseye one millimeter in diameter on the other side."

Dr. Turner's research focuses on the earliest moments of creation, and the noteworthy point as it pertains to this book is this: *There is a precision that undeniably indicates that there is an order at work, in my life and yours, that goes beyond our understanding.* Mathematics strives to understand it. Physics endeavors to decode it. Religion seeks to explain it. Despite humankind's best efforts for the past thousands of years— and for thousands of years to come—*we simply cannot, and will never, get our minds around such perfect order.*

I bring forth the work of another notable physicist, John Wheeler. Dr. Wheeler served as a professor at Princeton University and was a young contemporary of Einstein. Wheeler devoted his work to what he deemed "deep, happy mysteries"—and he said this regarding the fine-tuning of the universe: "To my mind, there must be at the bottom of it all, not an utterly simple equation, but an utterly simple IDEA. And to me that idea, when we finally discover it, will be so compelling, and so inevitable, so beautiful, we will all say to each other, 'How could it have ever been otherwise?'"

While science attests to the notion of perfection in the construct of the universe, psychology brings things a step further.

Noted psychologist, Carl Rogers, taught that there is only ONE therapy. He stated that there is within the human condition only one thing that is truly therapeutic—and that is to *fill a room with LOVE*. To Rogers, the therapist's single job in bringing forth healing was a dissolving of separation from love. It is to fill a room with UNCONDITIONAL, POSITIVE REGARD.

Perhaps the reader finds the concept of love to be outside the appropriate boundaries of this book. You may ask, "Is it of import to discuss such a lofty topic as love when we are simply interested in the acquisition of business and wealth?"

When you next read the original text of *Think and Grow Rich*, you will study men and women of considerable achievement who accumulated great fortune, fame, and influence. They are admired for their achievements, and rightfully so! But do we admire who they are? This author's contention is that great wealth and great character should not be mutually exclusive, and that when one is sought after at the expense of the other, we fall pitifully short of our full-potentiated self.

SUCCESS LEAVES CLUES, BOTH WAYS

It has been said that SUCCESS LEAVES

CLUES, but this does not mean that all the clues we find should be emulated. We must demonstrate an awareness and discernment of what aligns and misaligns with our highest self.

Consider, for example, the fascinating story of Steve Jobs, who built Apple as one of the greatest technology companies of all time and is known to this day as one of the greatest entrepreneurs in recent history. While Jobs' impact on the world is undeniable, his desire to succeed and his addiction to perfection caused him to also be remembered as a most demanding and malignant boss and leader.

He required, and some would say forced with the threat of termination, employees to work weekends and long hours, with *no regard for their personal and family lives*. If their work did not live up to his often-unrealistic expectations, he did not exercise restraint from insulting them or unleashing his anger publicly and in front of their peers. On one specific occasion, he laid off a group of Pixar employees without a two-week notice and without severance pay. When one of the workers requested that Jobs give them a two-week notice, he replied curtly, "Fine, but the notice is retroactive from two weeks ago."

Firing employees in a rude, inconsiderate,

and uncompassionate fashion was not a rare occurrence for the tech mogul. After his idea for a web-based email app failed, he fired the leader of the team in front of an auditorium filled with her fellow employees. In his speech, he proceeded to tell all of the employees who worked on the project that they had tarnished Apple's reputation and that they should despise one another for letting everyone down!

While some argue that this was simply part of his leadership style, Steve Wozniak, who was Jobs' business partner, said many of his compatriots at Apple claimed they would never work for Jobs again if given the opportunity.

Wozniak was not only co-founder of Apple, but also one of Jobs' best friends. This didn't stop Jobs from lying to him when the two created a game for Atari. After convincing Wozniak to work non-stop, for days, to come up with the ground-breaking game, Jobs cheated him by giving Wozniak less than half of what Atari paid. Additionally, Jobs kept the bonus from the business venture. Wozniak, who found out about the scandal years later, admitted to crying when he first learned about what happened. The technology genius may have created a business empire, but his LACK OF COMPASSION, EMPATHY, AND LOVE caused both his employees and friends to feel hurt and belittled.

Jobs undeniably accumulated great wealth and made many others incredibly wealthy; yet, the question I posit to the reader is this: *Does this story paint to you a picture of the person you want to be? Is it reflective of your highest values?* The creative faculty inside you is one that you have sought to make more alert and receptive to the vibrations around you—what vibrations do you sense upon reading this story?

This story is not recounted to malign Jobs or any other leaders, tycoons, moguls, or gurus of the sort. Rather, it is told out of a desire to help you practice SPIRITUAL HYGIENE— to point out that when we speak of becoming our full-potentiated self, we must take into account all aspects of our being, not just our bank statement or portfolio.

History affords us the opportunity to learn from both the great successes of others as well as their shortcomings. Perhaps you may not be a globally recognized figure like Jobs, Buffet, Carnegie, or the like. But what will history say of you? What will your family say? What will your closest associates, who in many cases may have helped you grow your very own empire, say about you? If there be any pricking of your soul as these questions are presented to you, I dare say this is your heart attempting to tune into the frequency of LOVE!

Great tragedy has an unparalleled ability to bring to the surface the innermost desire of the human soul. Faced with the last moments of their lives, the men and women trapped in the World Trade Center in New York City during the September 11 attacks did not phone their stockbrokers or rearrange their portfolios. Financial assets were not at the forefront of their minds! They called their families and simply said, "I love you."

HOW TO BECOME A PERSON OF LOVE

No amount of riches, adulation, achievement, or status will ever come close to the fulfillment that comes from being and becoming a person of LOVE. Becoming a person of love develops incredible inner strength.

LOVE is attracted to the one whose heart is favorable to it in the first place. Huge numbers of people make mistakes in relationships and go through life miserable and unhappy because they fear the pain that may follow if they open their heart. Countless numbers of men and women, both young and old, permit fear to ground their lives in the name of safety, stranded because they are afraid to leave the shore. People refuse to take chances in becoming a person of love, because they fear others will take advantage of them. "Don't aim so high; that kind of relationship is for the movies, or everyone else—not you."

Has your mind ever created alibis and excuses like this? All of them are traceable to FEAR. As you will find is mentioned in the chapter on the SIX GHOSTS OF FEAR in the original text, one of the core fears of men and women alike is the loss of love, and this fear drives us to withhold our love, which is the greatest gift we can give. And yet, to experience love means to love others and love ourselves. What does this involve? There are four things:

- First, we must to be able to process our own understanding about the human experience and have an understanding and empathy for each other's needs. As we give space to ourselves to acknowledge that this thing we call life is indeed a process through which we are always moving and never arriving, this naturally creates a space of grace to those around us to also be in process, and to be okay with that.

- Second, we must be able to have compassion and patience. It is said that love is patient—something that I struggled with greatly on my own journey of self-awareness, and still need to daily keep in check lest it take me off track during the difficult moments that can arise in any human interaction. Patience is a virtue, which, by definition, is a behavior showing high moral standards. In other words, as we increase our self-awareness, it leads us to a heightened degree of discernment in how to best conduct ourselves and relate to others, and with that comes greater degrees of patience toward those around us.

- Third, we must remember that none of us really knows each other's stories (a principle taught in the chapter on forgiveness). We must remember the words of Stephen Covey and seek first to understand before we seek to be understood. When we allow another's voice to be heard and to feel heard, rather than attempting to drown out all others with our own declarations and ultimatums of right and wrong, we give to another that which they most desire: to feel important, valued, and ultimately loved. As we create that experience for another, we keep the original, meaning you cannot transfer these emotions without feeling them yourself.

- Fourth, we must keep in mind that our current understanding and capacity for love really just reflects the surface of what is possible for each one of us at our current level of willingness to grow. Simply by reading this book and participating in the study that accompanies it, you have opened the door to a heightened level of willingness to make more love available to you as it also flows through and from you. Well done, my friend!

When we speak of experiencing love, we must understand both HOW WE PREFER TO RECEIVE LOVE AND HOW OTHERS PREFER TO RECEIVE LOVE. This gives us openness to the capacity of speaking the language of love to others we care about. To do so requires that we learn to give the "benefit of the doubt" and believe that every person we encounter has positive intentions—regardless of how skilled (or unskilled) they are at showing it! We suspend judgment and cease labeling people with our opinions of how they're acting. WE SEPARATE A PERSON'S BEHAVIOR FROM THEIR BEING, as I shared in the chapter on Forgiveness. I teach this principle in my Turning Point Retreat, and I describe it as "declaring noble intent first." The starting point is not one of negative judgement, but rather declaring the other person's intent to be noble, at least to their own level of self-awareness.

It is not possible that you will ever know every person's full story. Becoming a person of love relinquishes the need to know the story. If compassion is contingent on knowing the story, then only a few will ever prove themselves worthy of your compassion. That is, in fact, a very low amplitude of compassion and awareness. The higher degree of compassion involves opting out of the decision to be compassionate! *It is simply TO BE COMPASSION itself*: to start from and with the spirit and frequency of love.

Perhaps this sounds idealistic to you! Each one of us encounters the human experience every day. We come across a person whose behavior is rude, or we get cut off in traffic by a person whose behavior is inconsiderate. A friend gossips about us, or we're mistreated in the workplace. But what kind of frequency are you living from when you live at a level less than one of LOVE? Can the universe bring opportunities, people, and experiences to you when you are living on a lower-than-average plane? What do you do when you encounter people whose behavior is less than loving?

Do you react in an "eye for an eye" manner, or do you choose to respond from a higher level of awareness and to respond from and with love?

It should be noted that I have not once stated that becoming a person of LOVE has anything to do with how others treat you. As in every other chapter in this book, the transformation starts with you, and it starts from within the heart. This has everything to do with how you treat others. Many a person will say, "I will become LOVE when I am first LOVED." The question I had to ask, and still continue to ask, as a person who remains "in process," is this: "Did GOD not love you first? Did not the universe conspire in an almost unimaginable and improbable fashion, from billions of possible outcomes, to bring YOU INTO THIS WORLD, and not another who would bear your name, your likeness, or your soul? Is it not love that the universe gave you the most precious gift of all, the most precious form of richness: LIFE?"

Still, some will retort, "Yes, but I want HUMAN love. I want someone to shower me with affirmation, and calm my fears, and assure me that I will not be hurt, or harmed, or tossed aside—and that I will now and forever be of value." Truly, for one to meet all those criteria for another would require them to be a divine being in the first place!

We do not become people of LOVE simply because another person loves us. Love from another can surely open our hearts—and it is vital to understand how we prefer to be loved. Yet, to be open to love and to BECOME a person of love are entirely different matters. To become a person of love begins with UNCONDITIONAL love toward others. The focal point is on what you can give—for it is then that you operate out of your inner source, which is connected to, and one with, the creator and master of all love, God. This is why I have shared with you the missing chapter on TITHING, which is the act and commitment of giving from the vibration of love.

Allow me to pose several questions to you. I recommend you consider your answers both now and in the days to come. You will see that by answering these questions both fully and truthfully, the power to transform yourself into a person of love is SOLELY WITHIN YOUR MEANS.

- How can I appreciate, and show my appreciation even more for, the love and connection with others around me?

- How can I appreciate, see, and be aware of even more the perfection of this moment?

- What is the best thing I can do right now to express love and to connect myself with others?

- How can I open my heart more to happiness by seeking to love and connect with others?

All of these questions are questions of willingness and awareness, and all of the answers to them are a "you and you" deal. They require and demand nothing from another person, but rather can and should simply be unconditional.

This is not meant to be a lofty, grandiose exercise. The key here is to simply understand and acknowledge that "I move toward LOVE when I ____." The emphasis is on "I" and not on "my spouse" or "my friend" or "my boss" or "my child." For example, I MOVE TOWARD LOVE WHEN I GIVE MY PRESENT COMPANY MY FULL ATTENTION AND PRESENCE."

Fill in the blank with even the simplest of deeds! Is it to play with your children? Is it to listen with intent to truly hear the other person? Is it to bestow a gift upon a friend, colleague, or loved one? The power to move toward love is solely your prerogative. It is the act of tuning YOUR FREQUENCY to the highest one that exists in the universe.

THE SIX LOVE SUPPLIES

Considerable research has been conducted on what makes a person feel loved. One of the best ways that we can begin to generate a higher experience of love's presence in our lives is to imagine what it would be like speaking with somebody who only spoke a foreign language. We would either want to learn a few foreign words, or we would want to have a translator so that we could have mutual understanding.

The analogy is the same when it comes to the language of love. Each one of us can become more fluent in our ability to express love in the ways that serve the people we care about. These are the Six Love Supplies (several of which were made famous by the author Gary Chapman in his work, *The Five Love Languages*):

1. Being Listened To
2. Receiving Praise and Acknowledgment
3. Physical Touch
4. Being Supported In Goals and Dreams
5. Receiving Loving, Constructive Feedback
6. The Keeping of Agreements

In studies to discover what makes a person feel loved, BEING LISTENED TO

POWERFULLY AND DEEPLY was the most popular response. Listening is the place of connection. Most of us have been poorly trained in the art of listening! We plot and plan our responses before we've even finished hearing the other person speak. When we seek understanding without requirement of anything from the person speaking, and when we increase the level at which we authentically listen to even the people we know best, we supply them with EMOTIONAL OXYGEN.

Second, there is always something we can find to PRAISE AND ACKNOWLEDGE in another. Consider the person who consistently and sincerely greets others by saying something nice about them. They are often influential and referred to by others as a great leader, manager, friend, spouse, and so forth. A key step in making this a habit in your life is to CATCH PEOPLE DOING SOMETHING RIGHT. We are so accustomed at catching what people do wrong that the very notion of catching someone doing something right will feel completely foreign to us.

Taking this approach tasks you with becoming a NOTICER, and it attunes you to the vibrations around you, helping you develop insight and appreciation. Do not become discouraged if you cannot do this upon the first attempt. As you proceed to read the original work by Hill, you will see in subsequent chapters that the subconscious mind may be voluntarily directed *only through habit*. Be persistent.

The third most popular way of being loved is through PHYSICAL TOUCH—this can refer to a warm hug, a touch, a kiss, or sexual intimacy. These should obviously be exercised in their proper context. A word of advice here: When you shake someone's hand, BE IN THE HAND THAT'S SHAKING THE PERSON'S HAND. If you're hugging your spouse or your child, make sure you're fully present and appropriately engaged in the moment.

When we are not fully present, touch can become mechanical and rudimentary. All too often you'll see a parent pat a child's head, but the touch is devoid of presence and engagement. It is akin to someone smiling, but only with their mouth and not their eyes. What we are striving for is a real communication of caring, one that is always appropriate and in line with the moment. It is ALMOST ELECTRIC IN ITS ENERGETIC EXCHANGE. This is the kind of touch associated with the experience of being loved—when we feel an exchange of energy in that moment we are touched.

These are the first three of the six behaviors that became recognized in the research project on how people experience love. The next three have to do with supporting one another's hopes, desires, and dreams, how we offer our feedback, and keeping agreements.

The SUPPORT OF DREAMS AND GOALS is the fourth way people feel loved. It is no wonder, because as soon as an individual embarks upon his or her dreams, INDECISION, DOUBT, AND FEAR are apt to appear. It is stated in Hill's work (in Chapter Fifteen on the six basic fears) that the fear of CRITICISM is second only to the fear of POVERTY. When a person embarks on a journey to achieve their dreams, they immediately confront the fear of poverty ("Will I be poor if I do this?") and criticism ("Will people think me a fool?"). Turn the spotlight of LOVE and affirmation on a person and you will help them create thought impulses that will begin to translate themselves into their physical equivalent of success.

It has been stated that receiving FEEDBACK is the fifth way in which a person may feel loved—as long as it is done in a loving and constructive manner. When feedback is out of balance with just a taint of judgment, it isn't very loving at all. It feels like criticism, which, as stated in the prior paragraph, is one of the six basic fears.

Refrain from giving feedback unless you are one hundred percent committed to being accountable to the person. Pointing out a problem without the commitment to help that person evolve is in poor taste. What could be meaner than pointing out the buffet to a starving person, but not being willing to buy them a ticket to the feast?

When someone asks, "Will you give me your honest opinion?" take great stock in your decision. The reason is that most honest opinions are filtered through something that is not always the truth. THERE IS A DIFFERENCE BETWEEN AN HONEST OPINION AND THE TRUTH! A person can be very honest with you, yet not be in the truth of the situation. Many of my schoolteachers shared their honest opinions of me in front of my mother. They would tell my mother, "He will never make it academically. He will never be smart enough to earn a college degree. He won't even reach high school graduation. He'll never amount to anything. He will likely be reduced to a life of manual labor."

These were honest opinions based on very real facts—but, no, they were not my truth. All of the things to which they referred were the result of behaviors, and all of those behaviors were driven by my belief that I was dumb and stupid, the direct result of my childhood programming from an abusive parent and a home filled with physical and verbal violence. We can create nothing that we do not first conceive in THOUGHT! Had I not learned how to influence my own thoughts, these opinions would have embedded themselves deeply in my subconscious, and I would have manifested them in my life and my results forever.

Carefully guard your heart, words, and thoughts when asked by others to give your honest opinion. It may be honest, but it is still just an opinion and may not be their truth. Err excessively on the side of compassion and of having their best interests at heart. People pride themselves on being brutally honest. One should never be BRUTAL and, in fact, a person's brutal honesty, in the vast majority of cases, will merely be their own opinion.

Finally, there are AGREEMENTS. As we learn to be more and more skillful in our patterns of loving, we become very careful about the agreements we make and more rigorous with ourselves about keeping them.

Do not be casual about making promises and agreements! One of the integrity points of stable and solid relationships is the foundation of an agreement being kept. Breaking someone's trust is like crumpling up a perfect piece of paper. You can smooth it over, but it will never be the same again.

There is perhaps no greater source of joy, fulfillment, sorrow, and pain than the area of human relationships. All of our emotions—love, passion, joy, frustration, fear, and more—are intensified in human relationships. There will be moments when you have an opportunity to participate in a LIFETIME MOMENT with someone. Your actions in that moment can make a lifetime impression of what LOVE looks like in human form: how it listens, how it praises and acknowledges, how it moves through touch, how it supports dreams and goals, how it offers loving feedback, and how it keeps agreements.

This is really our journey: to learn to live ever more fully from the aliveness that is of the Infinite Source, and to love our neighbor as ourselves, which then dissolves all separation. It has been said that faith, hope, and love remain, and the greatest of these is love. LOVE is worth the effort.

Now, as we close out these chapters, I ENCOURAGE YOU TO CONSIDER the original text of Napoleon Hill's classic *Think and Grow Rich*, and you shall see how these three missing chapters, and the spiritual principles within, BRING FULL LIFE AND COMPLETION TO THE CLASSIC WORK, so that you, the reader, may live into the full richness of life that is available to you.

– The End –

If you have enjoyed this book and would like to learn more, join Paul Martinelli in a guided study and get your free copy of the original text of Napoleon Hill's classic, *Think & Grow Rich*.

Visit **TheMissingChaptersBook.com**

Made in the USA
Monee, IL
04 February 2020

21298498R00075